DK READERS
Level 2

Level 3

A Note to Parents

DK READERS is a compelling program for beginning readers, designed in conjunction with leading literacy experts, including Dr. Linda Gambrell, Distinguished Professor of Education at Clemson University. Dr. Gambrell has served as President of the National Reading Conference, the College Reading Association, and the International Reading Association.

Beautiful illustrations and superb full-color photographs combine with engaging, easy-to-read stories to offer a fresh approach to each subject in the series. Each DK READER is guaranteed to capture a child's interest while developing his or her reading skills, general knowledge, and love of reading.

The five levels of DK READERS are aimed at different reading abilities, enabling you to choose the books that are exactly right for your child:

Pre-level 1: Learning to read
Level 1: Beginning to read
Level 2: Beginning to read alone
Level 3: Reading alone
Level 4: Proficient readers

The "normal" age āt which a child begins to read can be anywhere from three to eight years old. Adult participation through the lower levels is very helpful for providing encouragement, discussing storylines, and sounding out unfamiliar words.

No matter which level you select, you can be sure that you are helping your child learn to read, then read to learn!

LONDON, NEW YORK, MUNICH,
MELBOURNE, and DELHI

Senior Editor Victoria Taylor
Designer Sandra Perry
Senior Designer Anna Formanek
Design Manager Nathan Martin
Managing Editor Laura Gilbert
Publishing Manager Julie Ferris
Publishing Director Simon Beecroft
Pre-production Producer Rebecca Fallowfield
Producer Melanie Mikellides
Jacket Designer Jon Hall

Reading Consultant
Dr. Linda Gambrell PhD.

First American Edition, 2013
15 16 17 10 9 8 7 6 5

Published in the United States by DK Publishing
345 Hudson Street, New York, New York 10014

Page design copyright © 2013 Dorling Kindersley Limited

LEGO, the LEGO logo, the Brick and Knob configurations and the
Minifigure are trademarks of the LEGO Group.
©2013 The LEGO Group
Produced by Dorling Kindersley under license from
the LEGO Group

Copyright © 2013 DC Comics
BATMAN and all related characters and elements are
trademarks of and © DC Comics
(S13)
DOR28811

012 – 187447 – Feb/13

DK books are available at special discounts when purchased in bulk
for sales promotions, premiums, fund-raising, or educational use.
For details, contact: DK Publishing Special Markets, 345 Hudson
Street, New York, New York 10014   SpecialSales@dk.com

A catalog record for this book is available
from the Library of Congress.

ISBN: 978-1-4654-0176-2 (Paperback)
ISBN: 978-1-4654-0177-9 (Hardcover)

Color reproduction by Media Development and Printing, UK
Printed and bound in China

Discover more at
www.dk.com
www.LEGO.com

Contents

DK READERS

BEGINNING
TO READ ALONE
2

DC UNIVERSE™ LEGO SUPER HEROES

SUPER-VILLAINS

Written by Victoria Taylor

Batman   Robin

The Heroes

The world's super heroes have got a lot of work to do. They must keep the crime-filled streets of Gotham City and Metropolis safe.

There is a frightening group of super-villains causing havoc! They enjoy making things as difficult as possible for the super heroes.

Wonder Woman

Superman

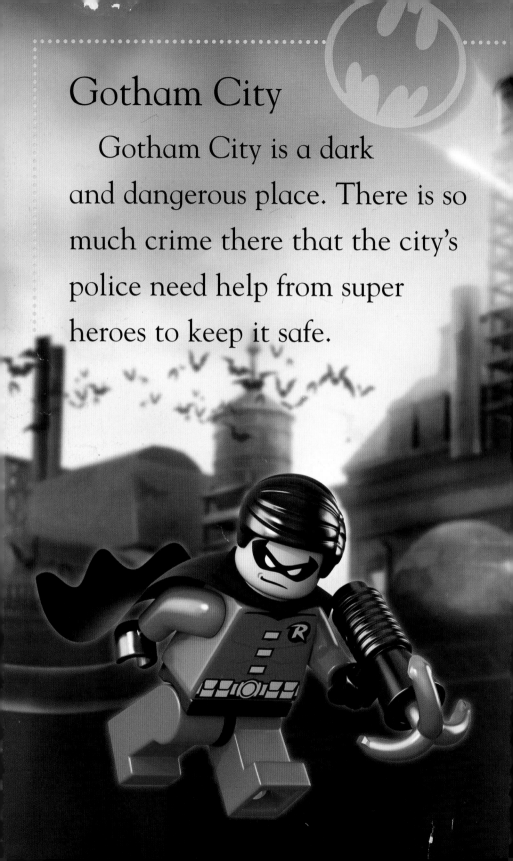

Gotham City

Gotham City is a dark and dangerous place. There is so much crime there that the city's police need help from super heroes to keep it safe.

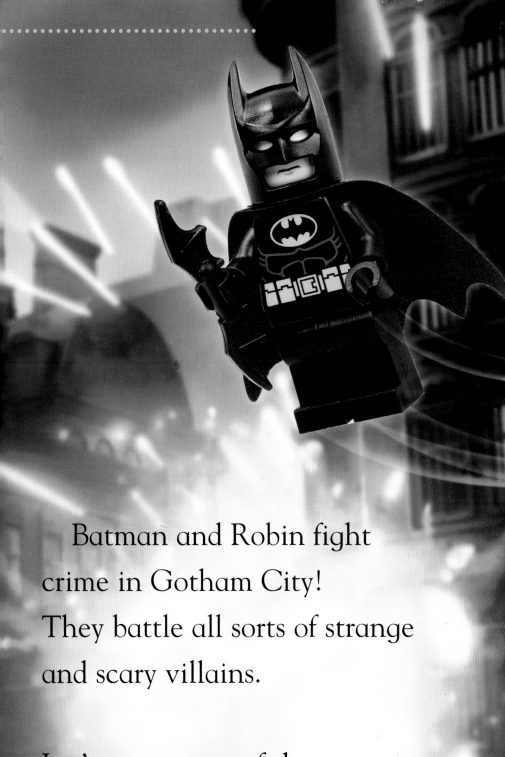

Batman and Robin fight
crime in Gotham City!
They battle all sorts of strange
and scary villains.

Let's meet some of them . . .

The Joker

The Joker is one villain that Batman does not find funny! He has a white face, bright green hair, and a permanent smile.

The Joker does not take being bad too seriously. He has all kinds of joke-themed weapons and gadgets.

He loves to surprise Batman whenever he can. Bang!

Mr. Freeze

Mr. Freeze enjoys doing battle on ice!

He likes cold, snowy conditions that match his frosty personality.

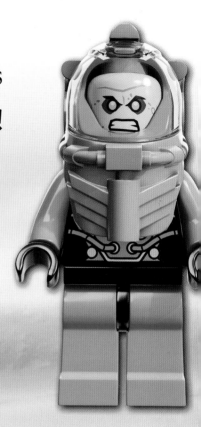

He can turn his enemies into blocks of ice with a freeze pistol that freezes them on the spot.

Luckily, Batman is too fast for him!

Catwoman

Watch out! Catwoman is on the prowl. She loves to steal sparkly jewels.

Jewel

Catwoman can climb tall
buildings with ease. She wears
a black suit that helps her hide
from Batman and blend into
the night.

Catwoman's
Catcycle

Well-protected
Catwoman carries a
whip and wears a mask
to hide her identity
when stealing jewels.

Harley Quinn

Harley Quinn used to be
a doctor at Arkham Asylum.
She once treated the Joker there.

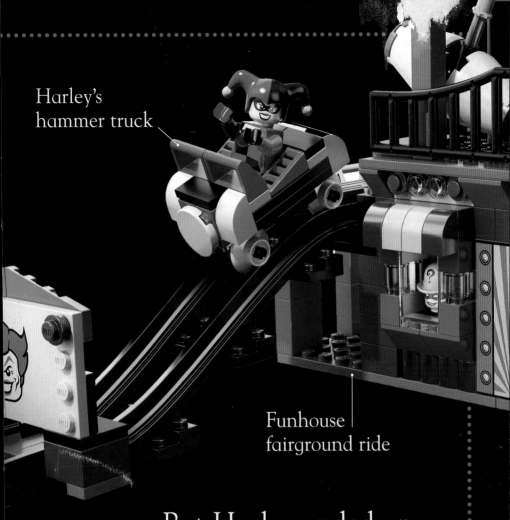

Harley's hammer truck

Funhouse fairground ride

But Harley ended up
forming a criminal duo with
the Joker instead of curing him
of his madness! The two villains
are on a joint mission to defeat
Batman once and for all.

Two-Face

Two-Face is double trouble.
He was in an accident that
turned him into the terrifying
villain Two-Face.
He is a master bank robber.

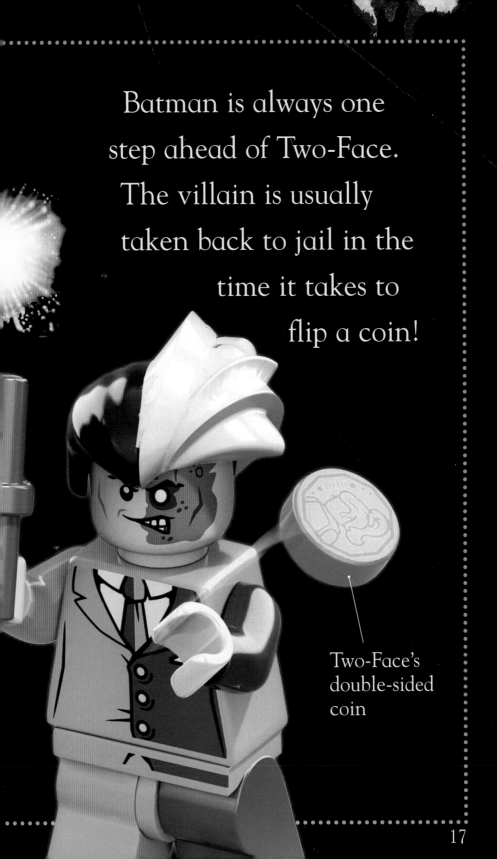

Batman is always one step ahead of Two-Face. The villain is usually taken back to jail in the time it takes to flip a coin!

Two-Face's double-sided coin

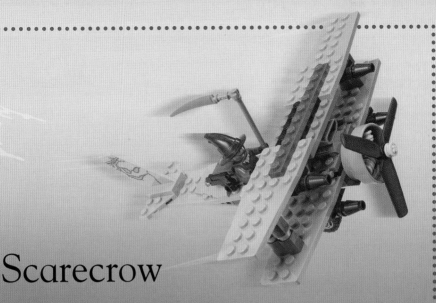

Scarecrow

Scarecrow looks terrifying
with his glowing red eyes.
He wears ragged clothes and
loves to scare people.

He flies an old-fashioned
biplane, which has four wings.

He might look horrific, but
Batman isn't scared of him!

Bane's Tumbler

Bane

Bane is one of the Batman's toughest enemies. He is very strong. He is also very clever and is good at planning his crimes in great detail.

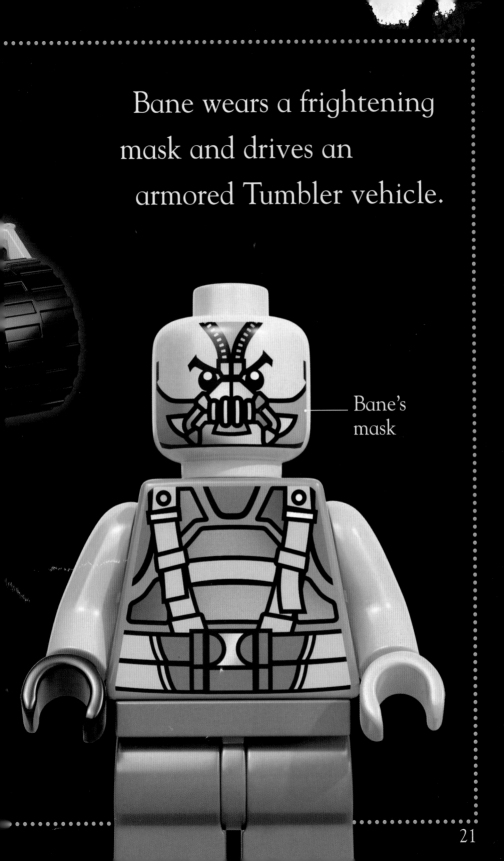

Bane wears a frightening mask and drives an armored Tumbler vehicle.

Bane's mask

The Riddler

Can you guess who this is?
It's the Riddler! He loves puzzles
and word games.
He even carries
a cane in the
shape of a
question mark!

Green suit

Question
mark belt

The Riddler always leaves
lots of clues about his crimes.
He loves watching Batman
struggle to solve his puzzles
and riddles.

Poison Ivy

Poison Ivy is one
of Batman's most
dangerous foes.
She has always
liked plants more
than people.

Poison Ivy uses
plant toxins to control the
minds of others. She wears
a costume made of leaves.

Vine

Poison Ivy has a whip
made from a vine.
She wants Gotham
City to become overrun
with wicked weeds.

ALERT!

HOLDING CELL

TEMP.

SCAN...

Poison Ivy
trapped in the
Batcave's jail cell

Metropolis

Batman and Robin have got Gotham City covered. Metropolis also has super hero protection against criminals and villains—Superman!

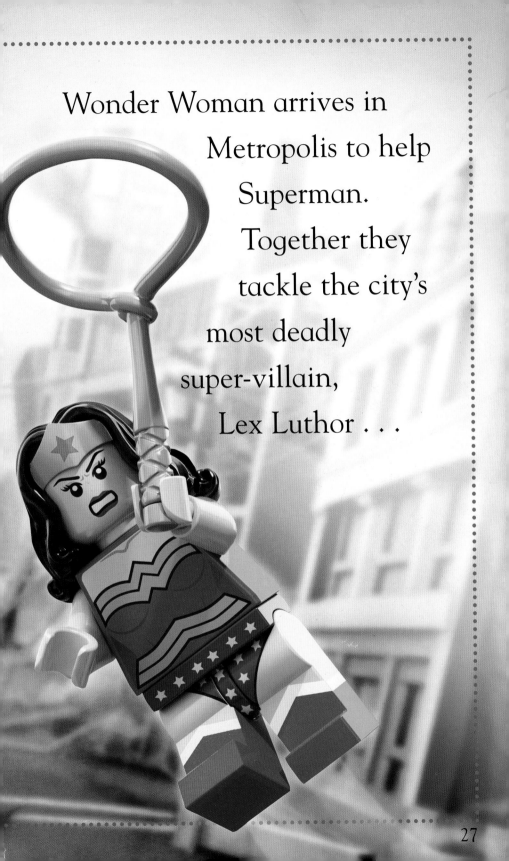

Wonder Woman arrives in
Metropolis to help
Superman.
Together they
tackle the city's
most deadly
super-villain,
Lex Luthor . . .

Lex Luthor

Lex Luthor has been Superman's enemy for a long time. Bald baddie Lex is a rich businessman and inventor.

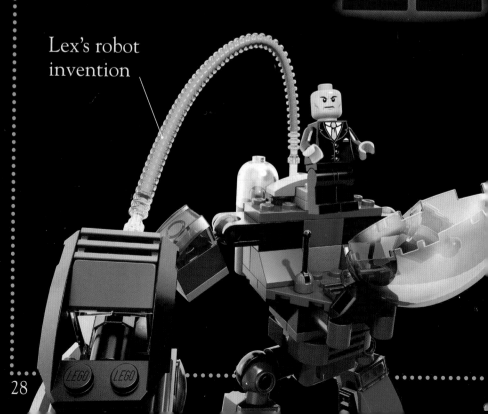

Lex's robot invention

Kryptonite gun
Lex invented a gun that
is powered by Kryptonite.
Superman becomes weak
when faced with
Kryptonite.

Lex loves to create his own
weapons and equipment to help
him to defeat Superman.

He has even invented a big
robot that he can sit inside and
control. It is super-strong but it
is no match for Superman and
Wonder Woman. He will have
to invent something else!

Locked Up

The planet's super-villains have many different powers and tricks up their sleeves. However, in the end they are no match for the super heroes!

The villains end up behind bars for their crimes.

Well done, super heroes!

Quiz

1. Whose weapon is this?

2. What is Catwoman's vehicle called?

3. What is this villain called?

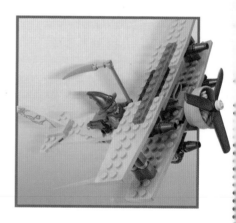

4. Whose biplane is this?

Answers: 1. Poison Ivy's **2.** The Catcycle **3.** Harley Quinn **4.** Scarecrow's

Index